ollins

C000001374

The Little Book of
Compost

Recipes for a healthy garden
and happy planet

Allan Shepherd

First published in 2007 by Collins,
an imprint of HarperCollins Publishers Ltd
77–85 Fulham Palace Road
London W6 8JB

The Collins website address is www.collins.co.uk

Collins is a registered trademark of HarperCollins Publishers Ltd

ISBN 978-0-00-726727-9

Editorial Director: Jenny Heller
Senior Editor: Lizzy Gray
Cover design and illustration: Emma Ewbank
Design: Bob Vickers

Printed and bound by Butler and Tanner, UK

The Menu

Dessert

Hot Californian Turnover 69
Have you got room for pudding?
Find out with this belt-loosening treat

The Drinks Menu

Compost Tea 85
Drooped without the brew?
Try this pick-me-up

Comfrey Cordial 91
Plant tonic – without the gin

The Wafer-thin Mint 99
To finish the meal off

Introduction

I'm not sure whether to liken the average compost heap to a Bacchanalian feast or a scene from a painting by Hieronymus Bosch. It's a dramatic carnival of life: the wildest party you'll ever throw; food, sex and death all mixed up in a fast-paced drama where the consumers become the consumed. A successful compost heap is a hot bed of fornication, consumption and defecation.

To borrow a phrase from Bart Simpson – Yoink!

If Bart were writing this there'd be no references to Roman feasts and medieval artists. He'd just come right out with it: compost is poo. There you go, Bart! The poo of millions of individual creatures who like to eat the stuff we throw away. *Ay caramba!*

If you've never made compost before, you may be thinking, Jeez he wants me to make a bucket full of poo. Yes I do, but this isn't the kind of poo you wouldn't want to step into; this is clean, beneficial, lovely poo that smells nice and helps our plants to grow. Poo to have pride in! That's a winning slogan if ever I heard one.

It pays to know about our poo-mongers: without them life, and therefore coffee, chocolate and strawberries, would cease to exist. They are the decomposers. Their job in the great scheme of things is to turn waste into nutrients for plants; without them our world would just be a sad old blob of rock in a stretchy universe. For all we know, like all of the others.

Our job as composters is to make life easy for the poo-mongers. All we need is a few simple recipes. This book contains eight of them. Like the classic cuisines, some of the recipes have been handed down for generations. Others are quite new, developed with a fresh scientific approach.

Human beings are the great compost chefs; we take a few basic ingredients, mix them together and create fertility. We can make nature work for us with no ill effect on the environment. In fact, through composting we can have a positive impact on huge numbers of garden species – ranging from the tiniest microscopic organism to the biggest tree.

So big yourself up. With compost you can make a difference.

Let's get this party started

Swinging parties don't make themselves. The skill of the host is in getting things right at the start. Do that and the rest will follow. Begin with the right combination of guests, a gourmet meal plan and a top-notch venue, and the party will kick off just as you'd hoped. With that in mind, let's start planning.

The Compost Gourmet

Most people assume compost is made in the garden, but actually the composting process starts on the chopping board in the kitchen, every time we peel a carrot, remove the husk from corn on the cob or skin a mango. If the waste from our Jamie Oliver recipes goes in a normal bin and off to landfill, the nutrients are lost forever. Worse than that, they fester and give off methane – a global warming gas twenty times more powerful than CO_2. If it goes back into the garden, the nutrients can go straight back into making more food. Good for gluttons everywhere.

Composting is an alien process to most people, but if you think of it as preparing a meal it suddenly becomes a lot easier; just another recipe to master. You don't even have to be a great chef. Imagine you're making food for organisms that need a good balanced diet to survive – um, just like a human being – and you'll be halfway there.

For humans the basic nutritional advice is to eat plenty of carbs and a small amount of protein. The same is true for most creatures that like to compost – though in composting we tend to use the words 'carbon and nitrogen' instead of 'carbohydrate and protein'. An overly protein- or nitrogen-rich compost heap ends up as a sloppy, nitrogenous, sticky mess no good to anyone. No place for the Atkins Diet here.

If we were making the perfect compost recipe we'd add one part of nitrogen to every 30 parts of carbon, but all materials that go in a compost heap have different ratios of carbon to nitrogen. For example, vegetable wastes have 12 parts of carbon for every one part nitrogen and paper has 170 parts carbon to every one part nitrogen.

From these proportions you can guess that vegetable peelings on their own won't make very good compost, but they work very effectively when they are mixed with some paper or cardboard. I'm going to talk much more about how this is done in detail later on in the recipe for Cold Turkey (pages 23–32) but this is a story I want to unravel slowly and we're not ready yet.

Golden Rule Alert
The browns and the greens

In composting, carbon-rich materials are generally referred to as 'the browns', nitrogen-rich materials 'the greens'. The browns are materials that are a little bit dry but full of substance – paper, cardboard, leaves, straw, woody waste and sawdust for example. The greens are charismatic, rich and quick to turn slimy, such as kitchen scraps from the chopping board, as well as grass and other weedy waste from the garden.

Here's a list of browns and greens to help you out:

Browns
- old straw
- tough vegetable stems
- herbaceous stems
- old bedding plants
- autumn leaves (in small quantities)
- woody prunings
- tough and evergreen hedge clippings
- cardboard and crumpled-up paper – stuff like egg cartons, loo roll holders, cereal boxes (especially the small variety pack boxes), fast food packaging and so on
- wood chip

Greens
- vegetable peelings
- fruit scraps
- tea bags and coffee grounds
- grass clippings
- young weeds and plants
- cut flowers
- soft hedge clippings
- nettles
- comfrey leaves
- rabbit hutch waste
- manure from chickens, goats, sheep, cows and horses

When you're making up a compost heap the golden rule is to add two parts green to every one part brown. Too much green stuff makes the heap slimy. Too much brown stuff makes it crackly and dry. Get it wrong and the stuff in your compost bin never becomes compost.

The guests

How difficult can it be? A few million round to dinner; a sprinkling of vegetarians; one or two who might start eating the poo of your other guests before the evening is out; and the odd couple of thousand deaths on your hands: nothing that a good host can't cope with. Think you're tough enough Mr Ramsay? Let's find out.

Here are five helpful tips for the perfect comp-host:

- **HOST TIP NUMBER ONE** – Most of our guests like air, apart from those you've invited to partake in the side dish Bokashi Sushi (see pages 47–54). These don't like air. Air-loving composters are called aerobic. Air-hating composters are called anaerobic. They don't get on so never invite to the same course.

- **HOST TIP NUMBER TWO** – All of our guests like moisture. Don't forget to provide enough water to keep them moist but not sodden through with dampness. Think sponge with most of the water squeezed out.

- **HOST TIP NUMBER THREE** – Most guests prefer a nice cool atmosphere, apart from those you invite to partake of the dessert menu. These like to eat in what can best be described as a sauna. Cool-loving composters are called mesophilic. Hot-loving composters are called thermophilic. They don't get on so never invite them to the same course.

- **HOST TIP NUMBER FOUR** – There are some rather large guests who like to crunch big bits of food. We call them the physical composters. They change the physical properties of compost – taking big waste and turning it into smaller waste. Some of these composters eat decaying stuff. Some composters eat the poo of larger creatures. Some eat each other. This little piggy went to market... They'll be there for the main course but they won't turn up for most of the others. Apart from the worms, which are, after all, the VIP guests for our side dish The Worm Stack (see pages 55–68).

- **HOST TIP NUMBER FIVE** – This apparent rudeness amongst your larger guests is not a problem. Most of the composting is done by guests you can't even see! 'You won't even notice we're here,' they say. These are the micro-organisms and they like to be called chemical composters. Nothing to do with nasty man-made chemicals. These composters change the chemical composition of our compost to make it plant-friendly and should be invited to every course. There are, however, several types of micro-organisms and some of them don't get on. The air-loving, cool-loving micro-organisms will be there for the starter, the main course, The Worm Stack and the drinking. The air-hating micro-organisms will be there for the side dish Bokashi Sushi. The air-loving, heat-loving micro-organisms will be there for the Hot Californian Turnover.

Venue

When you're throwing a party you expect to use more than one room. So it is with composting. Your guests like a variety of different locations. Some are quite happy in something confined and intimate

– like a bag or a bucket. Others prefer a nice open setting in which to express themselves – a compost bin, for example. Worms, being slightly fussy, like something specially designed for them. Every recipe comes with its own guide to making your guests feel at home. After all, if they're not happy, you're not happy. And smile.

Service

One problem with any party is knowing when your guests need to be looked after. Attend too much and your neurosis rubs off on them. Leave them completely to their own devices and they feel ignored. It's an age-old problem but one that can be overcome if you follow some time-worn advice. Of course, as you might expect, every guest is slightly different so for each recipe I have suggested an appropriate level of attention.

The Menu

This is an eight-course meal and you may find that you start to flag before the drinks. Remember, though, that you need not prepare everything on the menu. Your guests will be happy whatever you do, as long as you do it well. In my experience, the main course is the preferred dining option for most people, perhaps accompanied by a side dish, a drink or two and a nice wafer-thin mint to top the whole thing off. The starter is a little playful fun and the dessert something for those with the larger appetite.

I hope you will find that these recipes contain all the information you need to start composting, but of course there are always those who find themselves more excited about composting than there is room for in such a little book. For those people I have provided the Ideas Larder (see pages 105–109) – a store cupboard packed full of useful contacts, books and websites to explore. If you ever find yourself stuck for answers, raid the larder.

So now please join me in the kitchen and let's plan a meal.

Soil in the Bag

It's quick, it's simple, it's in a bag. This really is the TV dinner version of composting. It can be practised by the following people:

- • **THE HALF-ASSED IDLER** who wants to give composting a go.

- • **THE BIOLOGICALLY OBSESSED CHILD** who has moved beyond collecting tadpoles from their local park.

- • **THE SPATIALLY CHALLENGED HOUSEHOLDER** with a few plant pots, a spare bag of kitchen scraps and 30 seconds a day for composting.

Budget

A few pennies' worth of alfalfa pellets.

Equipment

One **medium-sized plastic bag** (recycle one from
the supermarket so long as it is watertight) and
a twist tie.

Ingredients

Vegetable peelings
Coffee grounds (optional)
Tea leaves (optional).
½ **cup of soil for starter micro-organisms** (not
sterile potting compost)
30ml (1fl oz) water
1 tbsp of **alfalfa meal or alfalfa pellets** (often fed
to hamsters or rabbits)

Guest List

Your guests for this course will be the air-loving,
cool-loving micro-organisms. They are the protozoa,
actinomycetes, bacteria, fungi, nematodes and algae.
Don't worry about remembering their names. You
don't cater for them individually but as a group.
Although it does of course make impressive
conversation at the dinner table.

Venue

A Plastic Bag: no holes in the bottom. This is a small little bag, so you can just about keep it anywhere. Put it in a drawer, any place you call a store. You can hang it on a hook, or keep it in a nook. Tie it on a rack or place it in a sack. Leave it in a cranny or lend it to your nanny. If it's going to wreck your marriage take it to the garage. (Apologies, Dr Seuss!)

Service

Low maintenance. Leave alone mostly. Your guests do however enjoy the occasional squeeze. See method for further details.

Preparation

To appreciate this recipe we need to get some angle on scale. If we think about composting creatures at all, most of us think fat visible worms, but most composters are so small we can only see them with an electron microscope – a big expensive piece of kit that magnifies the smallest detail up to about two million times its actual size. There are, of course, other large composters apart from worms and we'll get to those in due course. As this recipe is just for the little fellas let's hang out with them for a while.

Given the number of adverts for kitchen cleaning products that use the words 'wipe out harmful bacteria', most of us could be forgiven for assuming that bacteria wish us nothing but ill will. Embracing bacteria as a wonderful thing is akin to hugging a hoody, but there are plenty of beneficial bacteria and the compost heap has its fair share. They're the smallest of all compost creatures and it's easy to get excited about their size, the density of their populations and the sheer volume of activity that fills each working day.

If we took a small tweezer pinch of compost no bigger than the full stop at the end of this sentence and placed it under the lens of an electron microscope we could start counting the number of bacterial cells living there and be nowhere close to noting them all by the time we reached a hundred thousand. These creatures are so small and so much within their own world that if our compost-covered full stop was scuffed up by a child's foot or even blown into the air by the force of a bomb, the inhabitants would barely notice. This is why we can make compost in a bag. These guys have no concept of bag. They're just in compost heaven.

Method

Finely chop your vegetable peelings and pour them into your bag. Add coffee grounds and tea leaves if available. Add the soil. Add the water. Add the alfalfa pellets (these are high in nitrogen and help stimulate the composting process). Shake the bag vigorously. Return each day to give it a squeeze. Every other day leave the bag open to let the air in. If your vegetable peelings get too smelly they might be too wet or in need of more squeezing. Try adding a little bit of cardboard to soak up some water.

Serving suggestions

Add to any pot plants that would benefit from a little extra fertility.

Cooking time

Four to six weeks.

Cook's Questions

What does compost look like?

This composting method is just for fun, but whichever recipe you use you'll want to know whether what you've made looks right. How do you know that it's actually compost? Home-made compost never looks quite like the photogenic stuff you see on TV shows, so don't worry if yours doesn't look 'perfect'. The bulk should look like a dark rich crumbly soil, but don't be surprised if you find stray bits of uncomposted material in there too. You can just pick these out and add to the next lot of compost you make. If you want to know what compost should look like when it comes out of the bin the best website to go to is www.recyclenow.com/home_composting. Here you'll see a visual representation of the composting process, some great photos of what compost should look like during and at the end of the process and some good advice on what to do with the compost when it's ready – although I do offer plenty of serving suggestions throughout this book too.

Where do I get alfalfa pellets?

You shouldn't have a problem getting hold of alfalfa pellets. Pet shops should sell them as rabbit food. You can also get them from horsey websites, although they do come in rather large packets for a Soil in the Bag experiment. Try www.dengie.com/pages/products/additional-products/alfalfa-pellets (0845 345 5115). For something slightly smaller (a 907g bag), go to www.bunnybazaar.co.uk (0121 544 1511). Make sure you get 100 per cent alfalfa products.

Cold Turkey

This is the perfect recipe to go cold turkey on waste. Start composting and kick your addiction to the black bin liner. This is a slow composting method for the following people:

- **GARDENERS** who want to get all those nutrients from the kitchen back into their soil.

- **PARENTS** looking for a fun way of getting their kids in to gardening and recycling.

Budget
You can make a bin for free or pay anything up to £200. Most councils and some water companies are offering bins for around £10.

Equipment

One kitchen caddy (a bin to collect your kitchen
   scraps and cardboard)

Compostable bags (optional but they do cut
   down on cleaning. Just lift the bag straight out
   of the box and deposit on the compost heap,
   leaving the bag open to speed up the composting
   process).

Or you could just line your bin with **newspaper**,
   thus cutting down on cleaning and ensuring
   some carbon-rich material goes out to the
   compost heap with every caddy load of kitchen
   scraps.

One compost bin (or however many you require
   to deal with the level of compost you create).
   A second compost bin is a useful commodity.

A spade – for removing compost

A moisture mat (optional) – if you live in a dry
   climate, this will help to keep the moisture in
   the heap.

Ingredients

For nitrogen: selected kitchen scraps – vegetables,
   fruit, coffee grounds, tea leaves and bags (but
   not the don'ts – see page 38).

For carbon: cardboard – egg cartons, loo roll
   holders, cereal boxes (especially the small variety

pack boxes), fast-food packaging and shredded
documents.

Garden waste-nots – a good balance between
carbon-rich and nitrogen-rich materials. You can
use leaves, selected weeds, foliage and grass
clippings. See Cook's Questions for more help.

Compost crops (optional). See recipe for Comfrey
Cordial on pages 91–98.

Rabbit poo and **the poo of other herbivorous pets**
(but definitely not poo from cats and dogs – even
if they're kept on a vegetarian diet).

There are lots of other things you can put in a
compost heap, but I've only dealt with the materials
you will most commonly find around the home. If
you want a bigger list, check out the Garden Organic
website www.gardenorganic.org.uk or get hold of
The Rodale Book of Composting.

Guest List

This is the big bash. The Glastonbury of composting
– everyone will be there. All except the anaerobes,
but you don't need to worry about them, as they
can't contribute anything to a recipe like this. Your
guests will include all the air-loving, cool-loving
physical and chemical composters – the invisible
silent, chemical micro-organisms described in the

Soil in the Bag and the larger noisy crunchers. These include mites, woodlice, worms, springtails, nematodes, beetles, centipedes, millipedes and even what we consider to be unwanted guests at most garden parties – the ants, slugs and snails. Be prepared for some unexpected visitors too – the good, the bad and the ugly.

Venue

Whichever venue you choose, you should afford your guests lots of air and enough water to keep them nice and moist. Beyond that the choice comes down to taste and ambiance.

If you don't mind having an alien in your garden you can buy (and quite often get free from your local council) a bin that looks to all intents and purposes like a Dalek. Just stick a sink plunger on its chest and you'll see what I mean. These pre-formed plastic containers have a lid and quite often a little door at the bottom, from which to extract the finished compost. The lid's useful because it protects the heap from nutrient loss caused by excessive amounts of rainfall. I'm not so sure about the door. It does allow you to see if you're compost is ready, but if you want to get the compost out, lift the whole bin up. It's easier.

I'm a Glastonbury man myself. I like something open with a wall around it. My bin came from the Centre for Alternative Technology (CAT), who pioneered and tested this recipe with ordinary households and found that a simple square box with no lid worked better than any other compost bin (see the CAT factsheet Cool Composting at www.cat.org.uk/catpubs). If you want help making up your mind, check out the Cook's Questions (pages 32–35).

Service

Low maintenance. CAT christened this system of composting 'feed and forget' because you don't do anything to the compost once it's in the bin. So long as you've chucked in a good balance of browns (carbon) and greens (nitrogen), there shouldn't be a problem.

If your compost looks slimy, you need to add more browns. If it looks too dry, add more greens. The golden rule is two parts green to every one part brown. Use the list of browns and greens on pages 10–11 to help you out.

Preparation
A few top host tips:

- Place your bin on open ground (i.e. not on concrete patios) so composters can make their own way in and out of the bin – earth worms like to burrow when it's too hot in the heap. If it is not possible to site your bin on open ground, add a couple of spade loads of soil to get the microbes into the bin.

- Chuck in plenty of garden waste-nots as well. The Cook's Questions section on pages 37–46 has a complete round-up of what's good for the bin and what's not.

- Think about how much stuff you're going to put in the bin over six months and how much space you have for composting. If you don't have very much of either, you might consider keeping a wormery to compost your kitchen waste. You can keep these on a patio or, as many people do, inside the home or on balconies. If you have lots of ingredients to put in a compost heap, make sure you get a larger bin or a couple of normal-size bins. You can start one while the other is finishing and keep the recipe going all the time.

- The size of bins varies enormously, so make sure you're happy with the size you make or buy. Think about how the bin fits in with the overall look of the garden. You can get some very smart-looking 'beehive' bins. If you've got a small garden the last thing you want in it is something you think looks a bit ugly.

- Make sure you can get at your compost easily. Some bins make it hard to access the contents. Don't strain to move compost about. Composting should be light work, easy and fun. I wouldn't do it if it wasn't!

Method

Collect your kitchen scraps and cardboard every day in your kitchen caddy, and take up to the compost bin whenever convenient. Don't lay cardboard flat in a compost bin or tear it into little pieces. Instead, scrunch it into rough balls, somewhere between the size of an egg and a small melon. Compost creatures love the air spaces these crumpled cardboard balls provide. Add garden waste-nots whenever they come to hand, always balancing carbon- and nitrogen-rich materials. Do absolutely nothing else except, if you want to, study the activity of your compost heap wildlife. Six months later, you should have good crumbly compost. When you empty your bin, you will find three layers. The top layer will be the stuff you have only recently put in, which will be barely digested. The middle layer will be half-digested. The bottom layer will be compost. Lift out the top two layers and put them to one side or in a second bin to continue the composting process. Dig out and use the finished compost.

Serving suggestions

• Use your compost in the veggie plot. Some people like to dig their veg plot over every year and get the compost into trenches 15–30cm (6–12in) beneath the surface of the soil. Others like to spread it like butter on a piece of toast. Charles Dowding, celebrated author of *The Natural No-Dig Way* recommends a 50mm (2in) layer of compost across the whole garden. This keeps the weeds down and the worms busy. They drag the compost down into the soil, which helps keep the soil aerated. He insists there is no digging in nature so we shouldn't do it either. I'd recommend getting hold of his book and a good growing guide such as *The Complete Book of Vegetables, Herbs and Fruits* by Matthew Biggs, Jekka McVicar and Bob Flowerdew or the *Encyclopedia of Organic Gardening* by HDRA (the organisation now called Garden Organic). There's also further information in my book *The Organic Garden* and on my blog www.compostlover.com.

• Use compost on your pot plants. Pot plants need topping up with fertility. Remove the top few inches of soil around your plants and replace with compost. Leave a gap between the compost and the stem. Compost is strong stuff and can damage the plant by scorching.

• Put compost round your trees and shrubs and any other plants in established beds and borders. A 5x10cm (2x4in) layer should do it.

• Make a potting compost. If you're growing seedlings in pots, you can make an excellent potting compost with your own home-made stuff. You do have to mix it up with other materials, though, as it's far too strong on its own. The recommended mix is one part compost, to one part topsoil, to one part sharp sand (available at garden centres).

Cooking time

Six months if you're composting over the summer months; longer if you're starting in the winter.

Cook's Questions

How do I choose a bin?

If you have absolutely no idea what compost bins look like you should head to the website of the government-backed organisation WRAP – the Waste Recycling Action Programme: www.recyclenow. com/home_composting. Here you'll see versions of the Dalek-shaped compost bins, the square bins and other things like wormeries, Bokashi and so-called food digesters. Food digesters are for people who want to compost all their food waste – meat and cooked food included.

Most of the bins on the site are made from recycled plastic, so they're eco-friendly too. The website also has a facility to type in your postcode to find out what special offers on compost bins are available in your area. My postcode came up with a £10 bin called the Compost Converter 330: a 330 litre bin that would suit the average household. You can also buy a range of kitchen caddies too.

What you won't see here is the Rotol 300 litre bin, given the coveted Best Buy award by *Gardening Which?* magazine. This is being given away by some local authorities for as little as £14, but you can buy it for between £25 and £35 from a green gardening supplier like www.greengardener.co.uk.

You also won't see any DIY or bought wooden bins. For DIY bins check out the section below and www.gardenorganic.org.uk/factsheets/gg24.php. For bought wooden bins, go to www.cat.org.uk/shopping and hit the garden products button, or www.recycleworks.co.uk, www.greengardener.co.uk and www.wigglywigglers.co.uk.

Choosing which bin to use seems to be mostly down to personal preference, but there are a few important considerations. An open wooden bin allows water and air to pass easily into the heap, and you really shouldn't have to do anything more to it. If your bin is closed, you may have to water it from time to time or take the lid off occasionally when it's raining. You might also have to make some air holes in the heap to keep circulation high. In conditions of normal rainfall, keeping a heap moist is not a problem if your bin hasn't got a lid. If you're worried about moisture retention in an open bin during a long dry spell, you can buy or cut your own moisture mat to lay on the top. This is usually made out of a hessian type material and allows rainfall to permeate from above but suppresses evaporation from beneath.

The disadvantage of an open bin is that some of the nutrients can be lost to the soil beneath, as it goes through the equivalent of a prolonged rinse cycle. Some people design planting systems around their compost bins so they move the compost each year and plant up the space left empty by the bin, thus taking advantage of all the nutrients that have been washed into the soil and the top layer of compost that's left behind on the surface. As nutrients from compost tend to stay locked in the soil for several years, this has obvious advantages in a small plot where you are using a four-course rotation (see pages 103–4).

If you find the idea of lifting a bin up to get at your compost troublesome, you may be better off getting a square bin with slats that can be removed easily or one with a big fold-out door. The Recycle Now website advertises the Thermo King 600 litre and the Komp 800 litre – both made out of recycled plastic.

How do I make a bin?

A simple DIY design can be downloaded from www.gardenorganic.org.uk/factsheets/gg24.php. This does, however, require some carpentry skills, so if you don't have any tools whatsoever you could go for one of the following no-thrills bins:

- **THE USED TYRE STACK.** Get hold of three or four unwanted tyres, stack them one on top of the other and fill.

- **THE WIRE PEN.** Get about three or four metres (10–13ft) of strong woven-wire fencing, bring the two ends together into a cylinder shape and tie with wire or chain snaps from an ironmongers.

- **THE ONE-TONNE BUILDER'S SACK.** This is the kind of sack you see full of sand on a builder's job or discarded empty in skips. Nab one and use it as a compost bin. Cut the bottom off so compost creatures can get into the compost easily. Push four wooden stakes into the ground (these could be long straight branches cut from your hedge or old broom handles) and attach a different corner of the bag to each stake. Make sure the bag is taut, with the bottom edges of the sides of the bag resting on the soil. You can re-create this method using bits of old hessian too.

If you've got a hammer, some nails and a saw, you can make the DIY pallet bin compost heap. Take four unwanted pallets. Arrange three of them as if you were building three sides of a courtyard. Attach them to each other using the nails so the bin stands up. Take the fourth side and fashion a removable fourth wall. To do this, cut the pallet in half so it connects to the other walls but is half the height. Then remove a few inches off each of the bottom slats of the pallet. This allows you to push the pallet into place so the top slats fit snugly against the ends of the two supporting walls. You can then attach the fourth wall using the nails. When you want to remove the compost, just prise open the door and shovel it out.

All of these bins do, however, have their disadvantages. The pallet bin is heavy to make and even heavier to move around. The bag bin is not long lasting or strong. The tyre bin is ugly and some people worry about possible contaminates leaching from the tyres into the compost. But for a quick easy fix, they all work. Of the four, the wire pen is probably the most convenient.

If you're into DIY, and have got a big garden, plenty of carpentry skills and lots of tools, get hold of *The Rodale Book of Composting*, which has several designs for belts and braces compost bins that will last till the sun turns black.

Can I compost meat, dairy and cooked food?

When placed in a handy presentation box in the garden these products send out an attractant to every rodent within sniffing distance. As we are never more than 6 feet away from a rat (or 8, 10, 12 or 20, depending which particular website you chose to believe), it's a good idea not to encourage them to get any closer, especially as they carry the rather unpleasant Weil's disease. For most compost systems it's best to keep meat, fat, bread and cooked food out of the bin altogether, and as an extra precaution wear gloves when you handle compost. You can create or buy compost bins that are said to be rat-resistant or rat-proof (such as a tumbler bin – see Turnover recipe on pages 69–80). You can also use a food digester or the Bokashi Sushi method (see pages 47–54) if you want to compost these products

– though each has its advantages and disadvantages
as I describe.

What else can't I compost?
Just as important as what you put in is what you keep
out. Don't attempt to compost any of the following:
• meat and fish scraps
• cooked food
• glass and tins
• dog faeces
• used cat litter
• disposable nappies
• coal and coke ash
• plastics and synthetic fibres
• large cardboard boxes
• newspapers
• any metals
For more information, see the How to Make Great
Compost section on the Garden Organic website:
www.gardenorganic.org.uk/ organicgardening.

What can I compost from the garden?

When you first start gardening it's difficult to appreciate how much garden waste-not you'll actually produce in an average year. It all depends on what sort of garden you own. The five main waste-nots from a garden are weeds; foliage from plants that have died back or become surplus to requirements; prunings from shrubs, bushes and trees; grass clippings; and leaf fall. Only some of these materials can be fed into 'feed and forget' compost so we need to go through them all one by one.

Weeds

Yes but. I've called this a 'yes but' because you can compost some weeds, but you have to be careful. For example, if you've got a patch of nettles, you can harvest the leaves and stems and put them in a compost heap. They are, in fact, a rich source of nutrients. However, it is best to keep the roots out, which may start to grow in a cool compost heap. This is also true of the roots of many hard-core perennial weeds. Some weeds, such as Japanese Knotweed, reproduce vegetatively – which means they sprout from a cutting (and, in the case of Knotweed, from the root as well) – and should be kept well away from a cool compost heap. You should also be careful putting weeds laden with seeds in a compost bin. Seeds can survive the cool composting process intact and come up in your vegetable patch the next year. Although you can kill all weeds when they're tiny seedlings if you hoe your vegetable beds regularly, this can add to the workload. It takes a while to work out which weeds are good and which are bad, but it's a good thing to learn.

There are alternative ways of composting difficult weeds. In his book *Weeds: An Earth-friendly Guide to their Identification, Use and Control*, John Walker suggests using an old potting compost bag, turning it inside out, puncturing it with holes and leaving the filled bag in a sunny place. The contents will rot in heat, turning into rich, dark compost within a year. He also suggests drowning perennial weeds in a bucket. Starved of air, they turn into a slurry-like liquid to be poured onto the garden.

The turnover compost techniques deal with these weeds in a different way, by cooking them (see pages 69–80), which is one reason why many gardeners prefer hot composting techniques. However, it is an art form and takes more effort, so if you've got perennial weeds and don't want to put them in the cool composting heap, dispose of them through a council green waste collection scheme.

Foliage (non-woody plant material)

Yes but no. This is mainly a yes, but there is a little bit of no in there too. Yes to things that are 'over', like broad bean and pea plants when you've taken the crop, and flowers that you've dead-headed (removed before they've seeded to keep the plant producing fresh flowers). Yes to foliage that has had to be removed because it is in the way (either shading other plants you wish to encourage, or creeping on to pathways), or because it has died down and looks unattractive. No to anything that might be diseased. Again, diseased material is best dealt with in a hot compost heap, removed off site or in some cases burnt.

Prunings

No. Woody prunings are the branches you cut from shrubs, bushes and trees to keep them tidy, short, shaped in a particular way or more productive than they would have been if you left them alone (like a fruit tree). Woody prunings are high in carbon and take much longer to break down, so you can't really put them in a cool composting heap. If you've got a small garden with hedgerows, fruit trees or bushes and plenty of shrubs, it's hard to find space for all this woody waste. Most people in this situation either chip the wood to make a mulch and use it around plants or as a material with which to make paths, or take it to the council green waste recycling skip. The chances are you'll only need a chipper or shredder one or two times a year, so you're probably better

off hiring one rather than buying (try
www.brandontoolhire.co.uk (0870 514 3391)
www.jewson.co.uk (0800 539 766) or look
in your Yellow Pages).

Pruning is generally a winter-time activity
(although there are seasonal variations such
as summer-pruned fruit trees), so set aside
a weekend to prune and shred. You could
also cut a few branches to use as small log
piles for wildlife. The logs will break down
eventually, but whilst they're doing so
they provide excellent feeding grounds and
shelter for frogs, decomposers and other
damp-loving creatures.

Grass cuttings

Yes. Grass clippings can go in a 'feed and
forget' system – though you have to
remember that they are high in nitrogen and
can make a compost heap slimy if you don't
balance them out with something that has a
higher carbon content. It's also best to avoid
putting them in big clumps. Mix them up
with your kitchen scraps and cardboard and
any leaves you might find in the garden.

What can I do with excess quantities of grass?

No jokes please. You can use grass effectively in the Turnover or mix them with leaves in a separate heap to make a quick compost. It takes two weeks to make a leaf and grass compost, so long as you chop and turn the mix every three days. You can also mix two parts grass clippings with every one part manure for another relatively fast compost, with no need to turn.

People with large lawns who cut regularly may find it difficult to process large amounts of grass clippings unless they build extra compost space and can find a regular supply of carbon-rich materials to go with them. Here are a few practical alternatives:

• Use them as a mulch. A mulch is a layer of organic material laid on top of the surface of bare soil to suppress weeds and keep moisture in the soil. Grass clippings can be laid 7.5–10cm (3–4in) deep to suppress most weeds.

• Use them as a green manure. A green

manure is a crop grown to boost
the nutrient levels in soil. They are planted
on bare soils, cut and dug back into the
soil, where they provide food for compost
creatures. Grass is not really a green
manure, but the clippings can be scattered
on the soil and dug in.

• Change your mowing regime. There is in
fact no need to remove grass clippings
from the lawn at all. Don't let the grass
grow more than 4cm (1.5in) between
mowings, then cut when the lawn is dry
and you can leave the clippings where they
fall. Many people have also started to use
so-called mulch mowers. These cut the
grass and then chop the clippings into fine
pieces so they break down quickly. Lawns
cut with a mulch mower invariably survive
drought in much better health.

Tree leaf fall
Yes. Leaves have a high carbon content
(40–80:1 depending on the leaves) and can
balance more nitrogen-rich materials in the
compost mix. Most of the leaf fall happens
in autumn but is usually spread over several

weeks if not months. Gather the leaves up and
add to the compost bin along with everything
else, but not in great thick layers. Make sure
the leaves are mixed in with plenty of
nitrogenous material.

What can I do with excess quantities of leaves?
Leaves are very versatile when it comes to
making compost. You can make a separate
heap and compost them specifically with a
nitrogen-rich material like manure (five parts
leaves to one part manure). Leaves don't have
enough nitrogen to compost sufficiently on
their own, but you can make a compost
alternative called leaf mould. This is less rich
than a balanced compost, but it does provide
a wonderful mulch and has an amazing
capacity for holding water. Make a bin using
some old chicken wire or a builder's sack (as
described on pages 35–7), gather the leaves
up and chuck 'em in. If you don't want to
compost leaves in a separate heap, or haven't
the space, just pile them up around existing
plants and let the worms do the rest.

Bokashi Sushi

It's Japanese, trendy and an acquired taste. This is the easiest and quickest compost method around, mainly because it isn't composting at all. What you get at the end of the recipe is a mass of fermented material that can be added to a compost heap or dug into the ground. Only then will the true composting process begin. It is suitable for the following people:

- **THE COMMITTED MEAT-EATER** who wants to compost all their food scraps.

- **THE EXPERIMENTAL COMPOSTER** who wants to give it a go.

- **PEOPLE WHO LOVE ALL THINGS JAPANESE.**

Equipment

Bokashi bucket, or any bucket with an air-tight lid, a drainer and a tap.

Recycled container (i.e. jam jar, margarine tub) in which to collect primordial soup, otherwise known as Bokashi juice.

Ingredients

Left-over kitchen scraps from any meal – cooked food, meat and dairy included.

Bokashi Active Bran (you can get this from a green garden supplier like CAT and Wiggly Wigglers, but also check out the podchef on www.youtube.com making his own).

Guest List

There's a high chance these guests will get pickled, but unlike most guests with an eye on the bottle you don't have to lay on extra sauce. They'll create their own. These are anaerobic bacteria that ferment without air. Being a rather rowdy alcohol-sodden brew crew they don't get on so well with the clean-living aerobic crowd. It's best to keep them in a sealed container somewhere out of the way. Once you've closed the lid they'll just get on with it. Let them have a ball for two weeks and then turf them out.

The makers of Bokashi prefer to call them Effective Micro-organisms (EMs for short). I'm not quite sure what this means as there is no such thing as an ineffective micro-organism, but I'll let that one pass as effective marketing (EM for short). The EMs are a carefully controlled mix of bacteria, yeasts and fungi. Because it's difficult to apply them directly to compost they are generally added to a dry bran and molasses mixture which is then shaken over the top of the compost as if you were topping off a cake with a dusting of flour.

Venue

Part of the deal with Bokashi seems to be that you need to buy a patented Bokashi bucket. This may be effective marketing too, but the bucket does allow the process to work smoothly (although I did find users on an internet chat room who were getting by fine without it). Food is placed inside the bucket on a drainer near the bottom. The Bokashi drainer is there to allow the liquid run-off associated with Bokashi to pass through to the sump beneath. From here, it can be drawn out of the bucket by use of the tap. This liquid is packed full of EMs and nutrients from food waste and can be used as a green fertiliser for plants – it is said to be so powerful that just one teaspoon is added to every two or three litres of water. Bokashi is very different to most domestic composting recipes because it attempts to create compost without oxygen. EMs effectively pickle the contents of your bin. In fact, they do this best over a period of 14 days once the bin is full. So you need a second Bokashi bin to keep the whole operation working smoothly. Fill one bin up. Leave it pickling in the corner for a couple of weeks. While it's sitting there, fill the second up. And rotate.

Service
Low maintenance. In fact, your guests prefer to be totally neglected. Close the lid and let them get on with it.

Preparation
After two weeks, dig a trench in the garden, take the fermented contents of your bin, and fill. Alternatively you can add it to the compost heap.

Method

Get your bucket. Chuck in a layer of kitchen scraps 3–4cm (1¼–1½in) thick. Sprinkle on a handful of Bokashi Active Bran (BAB). Add another 3–4cm (1¼–1½in) layer of kitchen scraps; and another layer of BAB. Squeeze as much material as you can into the bin. Close the lid tightly so no air is allowed to pass into it and leave sitting quietly in some unassuming corner of the kitchen for 14 days. Don't forget where you left it! On the 15th day, pick up your bin, march it out to the garden and chuck it in a trench; or on your compost heap. Return to the kitchen, wash the bucket out and start all over again.

Serving suggestions

Bokashi has to be put in the ground or on a compost heap for further decomposition. It cannot be used as normal compost because it isn't compost.

Cooking time

14 days in the bin and then 2-3 months in the ground (or longer in a cool compost heap).

Cook's questions

Do I need Bokashi if I'm only going to compost my vegetable scraps and cardboard?

Bokashi is advertised as a solution to the problem

of what to do with cooked foods and meat and dairy products. There are two things to do with 14-day-old Bokashi compost – bury it or put it on your normal feed-and-forget compost heap. You might not be happy about doing this.

You may also not want to have food waste sitting around the kitchen for 14 days, although I should add there is no smell when the lid is closed. The liquid you draw off from Bokashi does smell – like rancid vinegar. It is the only composting method described in the book that smells. If you get a bad smell in any of the others you know it's gone wrong. Not in Bokashi. It's meant to smell like that.

When you empty the bin you have two issues. The first is catching the drainer when you pour the stuff out into your compost heap. It slips in there with everything else and can be difficult to fish out if it's been eaten by your Dalek. The other is cleaning the bucket afterwards. I'll leave you to ponder that one. Unlike the compost caddies you can't (as far as I know) get a compostable Bokashi bag to sit inside the bucket. You don't add cardboard to a Bokashi bucket, so what you're gaining in recycling all the cooked stuff you're losing by not putting in the cardboard. However, you can keep a separate caddy for the cardboard and take it out to the compost bin. The final answer to the original question is 'no', you don't need Bokashi to compost separated kitchen scraps.

If you're not convinced Bokashi is for you, wait for the Garden Organic report to come out in 2008. I don't have a definite date so keep checking the website www.gardenorganic.org.uk. Better still join up as a member and they'll keep you informed (024 7630 3517).

How do I get started?

Bokashi starter kits tend to come complete with two Bokashi buckets and a bag of EM-filled Bokashi bran. All of the packs I looked at cost between £50 and £60 with varying amounts of starter bran. Try www.cat. org.uk/shopping, www.wigglywigglers.co.uk, www.recycleworks.co.uk and www.greengardener. co.uk. You have to order the bran in refill packs after the first lot is used up. Wiggly Wigglers will set up a regular delivery for you so you don't have to remember to re-order. A new packet comes in the post every two months. This costs about £25 for a year's supply. Recycle Works have a whole load of EM-related products both for the garden and the home at their new website www.emproducts.co.uk.

Are there other all-food composting systems?

There is a bin that digests food without turning it into compost. The Green Cone breaks food down into carbon dioxide and nutrient-rich water that drains into the soil. Although this deals with food waste at the home rather than sending it off to landfill, it's of very little value to plants or soils. You can't put garden waste into a Green Cone either, so it's not really a complete solution. The company that make the Green Cone are now marketing a much larger bin called The Green Johanna. It's from Sweden, which perhaps explains the Johanna. This bin is an all-food and garden composter and does create compost – though I should add you have to put two parts food waste to every one part garden waste. This isn't a very good ratio if you live alone and have a large garden, but it might work out if you've a large family with a small garden. There is a manual that goes with the bin, which the advertising makes clear has to be followed, and a turning stick. See www.cat.org.uk/shopping and www.greencone. com for more details (020 7499 4344).

The Worm Stack

This one is a deluxe composting method for the following people:

- **SOMEONE WHO IS NO LONGER CONTENT WITH WHISKERS** the family pet and wants a few thousand more animals to look after and perhaps even stroke.

- **THE BIOLOGICALLY OBSESSED CHILD** who has gone beyond the Soil in the Bag experiment.

- **THE SPATIALLY CHALLENGED HOUSEHOLDER** who has gone beyond the Soil in the Bag experiment.

- **THE COMPOSTING CONNOISSEUR** who wants to go that extra inch for a nice bit of poo.

Budget

You can buy a ready-made worm stack starter pack for £100 or make one yourself using recycled materials. If you go down the DIY route, you'll just need to spend a few quid on some worms.

Equipment

One wormery – this could be either a box or a stack, bought or DIY, with a tap (for drawing off worm juice to use as a fertiliser) or without a tap (for not drawing off worm juice to use as a fertiliser).

A bucket to keep your selected kitchen scraps in. Some people feed their kitchen scraps direct from the chopping board to the wormery, but if you prefer to collect it in the kitchen and cut the trip to the wormery down to a couple of times a week, keep a little caddy in the kitchen.

Thermometer (optional)

Moisture reader (optional)

pH reader (optional)

One specialist book on making and using a wormery (see directory); or excellent instructions from the retailer; or an active online support network of fellow wormery owners. If things go wrong, you may need to get a bit of specialist advice.

Ingredients

Selected kitchen scraps – vegetables, fruit, coffee grounds, tea leaves and bags, bread (moistened with water), rice, pasta, cakes and biscuits (moistened with water), cereal. (See 'Service' for a list of what to keep out.) Quantities depend on the type of wormery you chose, but best to start off with small amounts and build up slowly. Worms will reproduce quickly once a colony has found its feet, so you can start to put more food in later.

Bedding – Carbon-rich material that provides carbon for the micro-organisms which help worms to digest food. For this you can use bills you've been shredding to prevent identity theft, torn-up newspaper, or bought bedding material like coir (coconut fibre). Amounts of recommended bedding vary depending on who you talk to. *The Worm Book* suggests an average bin should be three-quarters full of bedding when you start.

One or two handfuls of garden soil. This provides grit for the worms and micro-organisms to help the composting process.

Worms – Don't pick earthworms from the garden – it won't work. Ask a specialist supplier for Tiger worms. Choose a quantity commensurate with the volume of food waste (a process described in Cook's Questions).

The Guest List

No doubt who's the star attraction at this bash. The worm is a mighty composter, chewing up one half of its own body weight in food every day and producing the most wonderful poo that gardeners could ever hope to get their hands on.

A worm has a wonderful digestive system, or perhaps it is better to say *is* a wonderful digestive system, because there is not much more going on than the basic functions of life. It consists mainly of one long alimentary canal that takes the food in one end, passes it through an ingenious system of digestion and deposits it out the other side in the form of what is coyly called a cast but is in fact poo.

This cast is full of micro-organisms still working away at decomposing the material that surrounds them. Welcome gate-crashers at the worms' party. They take the carbon-nitrogen ratio of a worm cast down to a level acceptable to plants.

There are those who try to gatecrash a worms' party, but you can keep them out by keeping some of their favourite food out (details in Service, see page 61).

You also have to be careful which worms you invite. Common and garden earthworms are fine in the soil; in fact, fantastic. Tunnelling up and down all day, dragging nutrients from deep soils and making them available to plants, but, oh, get them in a wormery and see how they complain. Just when a party starts to heat up, they want to leave. Fair enough I guess, they just prefer deep cool soils, but it does make them a bit unsociable.

What you need is an animal that can take the heat and knows how to party – the Tiger worm. Don't scrabble around in the soil all day looking for them, though. Send an invite through the post to a mail order company and they'll come direct.

Venue: The wormery

Worms are quite content to hang out in a cool compost heap doing their thing, but if you want to get the most worm casts per pound of kitchen waste your best bet is to buy or make your own wormery. This concentrates the effort of the worms in one place, allows you to adapt your composting style to their needs and gives you easy access to the finished product. Unlike some compost systems, there is no heavy turning to do and if you keep your wormery on a table no bending either. You can also watch the composting process easily and carry out your own Darwinian study if you find yourself developing a healthy interest. There's something very gratifying about worm casts. You can see the visible rewards of your (well actually their) efforts in a way that you can't with Bokashi Sushi.

Like Bokashi there is some argument about the benefits of buying a bespoke bin for your worms. There are some very nice bins out there costing about £100 and there is certainly something good about receiving a starter wormery pack through the post ready to go, complete with worms, bedding and a full set of instructions. Then again, you can do the job yourself for a few quid and reuse some things that are actually quite difficult to recycle (see the Buy or DIY option in Cook's Questions).

There is also some discussion about the merits of the design of wormeries. Wormeries tend to be entrepreneurial three-storey stacks or quiet square boxes. The stacking systems could be another case of effective marketing, but like the Bokashi bin these wormeries do work very well. But, then again, so do the simple square boxes, so it's probably a question of horses for courses.

Service

High maintenance. How many guests have you entertained that have issues with moisture, temperature and acidity? And then there's the food.

When you first look at the list of what needs to be kept out of a wormery, you're rather left wondering what can actually go in – barred items are citrus fruits, meats and bones, onion and garlic, heavily spiced foods, dairy products, eggs, oils and salts. Though, to be fair to the worms, only some on this list are there because they definitely don't like them: others appear because they attract unwanted visitors such as flies and rodents. However, as before, you can feed worms vegetables, fruit, coffee grounds, tea leaves, bread, rice and pasta. No problem.

Method

STACK SYSTEM – See Cook's Questions on pages 63–68. Whether you buy or DIY the process is basically the same. Also download podcast 81 from wormery company Wiggly Wigglers – www.wigglywigglers. co.uk.

BOX SYSTEM – Divide the box into zones and rotate the feeding every week. Start in zone one by laying down the bedding so that it takes up three-quarters of the space in the zone. Peel back the top couple of inches of bedding and slide the food in, along with the right amount of worms. When week two comes along, do the same in zone two, and so on through zones three and four. By the end of the fourth week the food in zone one should be unrecognisable as food and you can start the process all over again. Carry on until all the bedding has disappeared. Harvest your casts and start all over again with fresh bedding.

PREPARATION TIP – If you've got very big bits of vegetable scraps, it's worth cutting or grinding them up before they go in.

Serving suggestions

A worm cast is very special: in fact, perfect for gardeners. It balances the acidity in soil, carries a package of essential nutrients and contains a high percentage of that magical garden ingredient, humus.

Worm casts can be sprinkled on your soil, put in the bottom of holes dug for transplanted seedlings or specifically placed around the roots of plants that may need some extra wahahaaay as the growing season progresses.

Cooking time

Six weeks to four months depending on the
wormery, time of year, conditions, level of care.
Or not at all if all your worms die!

Cook's Questions

How do I make a recycled wormery?

The easiest recycled wormery I've come across is at
the Yalding organic gardens in Kent. It's made with
three fairly large polystyrene boxes – the type used
for packing vegetables or fish. Ask around your local
market for spares. Quite often, they're left at the
end of the day for waste collection, so it shouldn't
be a problem finding some. Each box usually comes
with a lid, but you only need one: discard the others
or use them as seed trays.

Make a hole at the centre of the bottom box, 2.5cm
(1 inch) wide. Place the box on two small columns
made of some scrap material like old wood, bricks or
concrete blocks. The hole in the bottom box allows
excess moisture to run out. Place a small container
underneath and then dilute the liquid that collects
and use as a plant food. It's powerful stuff – use ten
parts water to one part worm juice.

Take the second box and make seven or eight holes in the bottom. These holes are for the worms to climb up and down between the boxes so they need to be at least worm-sized. Place this box on top of the first. Take the last box, make the same number of holes and place on top of the second. Put the lid on top.

To start, place kitchen scraps and small amounts of scrunched-up (not flat) cardboard in the bottom of the box (or some shredded bills mixed with a few leaves) for bedding, along with 100 Tiger worms. Keep on filling with kitchen scraps and a little bit of cardboard and paper. When the box is full, place the next box on top of it and start filling it. When that is full, do the same with the top box. The worms will move through the holes between layers in search of food. By the time the top box is full of food waste, the bottom box should be full of worm casts. Take it out and empty the contents (being careful to lift any worms you dislodge back into the wormery). You can put it straight onto the soil or use it as part of a mix for potting compost.

For other DIY bin ideas have a look at http://whatcom.wsu.edu/ag/compost/Easywormbin.htm and *The Worm Book* by Loren Nancarrow and Janet Hogan Taylor.

How many worms will I need in a DIY wormery?
The advantage of a ready-bought system becomes obvious when you try to work out how many worms you might actually need to get the wormery going. Whereas a bought system has been designed with the optimum number of worms for the size of the bin, a DIY approach requires you to calculate how many worms you might need. This involves weighing your food over seven days, dividing by seven to give you an average amount of food waste per day and multiplying by two to give you the total weight of worms required. I guess it's not too big a hardship so long as you don't mind separating the food do's from the don'ts as you're going along. The other approach is to just take a wild stab in the dark and guess how many worms you'll need. However, this can lead to the unintended consequence of your wormery being a complete and utter failure. You have been warned!

What issues will my worms have with temperature, moisture and acidity?
Worms in a wormery slow down and speed up as temperature changes. The optimum level of activity happens in quite a small temperature range (between 23–24°C/59–77°F) although worms are quite happy between 15–25°C. If the temperature moves beyond

this region worms start to slow down dramatically, eating less and thus processing less waste. Below 10°C (50°F) and above 30°C (86°F) they start to suffer. Temperatures beyond this area can be fatal. Wormeries should be brought in during the winter or insulated well.

Conversely, in the summer they should be kept out of very sunny hot places where they will quickly dry out. Worms are 80 per cent water and although they can survive for days submerged in it they cannot survive a day isolated from it. Worms breathe by absorbing oxygen dissolved in water. As soon as their skins dry out they stop breathing. Moisture levels in a wormery should be kept between 70 and 80 per cent. You can monitor this by checking with a moisture meter.

You might also want to get hold of a pH reader. Worms, like most animals, prefer soil acidity levels that range between pH6 and pH8 and are happiest when soils are totally neutral. Conditions inside a wormery are quite liable to change if the feeding regime alters suddenly, so make sure you're wormery doesn't become too acid. If it does it will give you a clue: it will start to smell. Crushed egg shells can help restore the balance or a little calcium carbonate. If you're a regular gardener who uses garden lime or hydrated lime to lower the pH in your garden, don't do the same in the wormery. It's just too strong. www.wigglywigglers.co.uk sell a rescue pack if things go wrong.

How do I find out more about worms and wormeries?
Wiggly Wigglers is the number one place on the internet to get good information, support and products related to worms and wormeries. They provide a lot of free advice and information on their website www.wigglywigglers.co.uk and even produce a free downloadable weekly podcast, covering worms and many other subjects. Get episode 81, a video podcast on how to use their Can-o-Worms wormery. They also sell wormeries, worms, bedding and various other bits of kit you might need.

I'd also recommend getting hold of a good book about worms too. Try one of the following:
The Worm Book, Loren Nancarrow and Janet Hogan
    Taylor, Ten Speed Press
Worms Eat My Garbage: How to Set Up and Maintain
    a Worm Composting System, Mary Applehof,
    Eco-logic Books
Composting with Worms: Why Waste Your Waste,
    G. Pilkington, Eco-logic Books

These books are available from www.cat.org.uk/shopping along with many other useful composting books and products.

Why are earthworms so good for the soil?

Earthworms create amazing super highways in the soil. They love to take food from the surface of the soil and drag it deep underground – sometimes down six feet or more, way below the roots of many of the plants we like to grow. When they eat food at this depth they mix it up with nutrient-rich soils and bring the nutrients back up to the surface of the soil, where they are deposited in casts close to the roots of plants. It's nature's way of bringing buried nutrients back into use. Just as importantly, the tunnels created by earthworms facilitate the movement of air and water around the soil. Air and water are both vital ingredients for a healthy soil. The soil community can't survive without them.

Hot Californian Turnover

I'll leave you to guess what the turnover part means. The 'Hot Californian' bit is because it's hot and was developed at the University of California, dude.

There are actually quite a few variations to the Turnover, but I've gone for one method to give you a clear recipe you can follow. It is important that your heap is at least 1m (3ft) wide, 1m (3ft) long and 1.2m (4ft) high, so don't start a hot heap unless you know you have at least this much material to fill the space. It needs to be this big to create the critical mass of heating necessary to work properly.

This recipe is for:

- **COMPOSTERS WHO JUST CAN'T GET ENOUGH**

- **OBSESSIVE DUNG-HUNTERS**

- **THE COMMITTED RECYCLER**

- **THE KEEN GARDENER** with a large garden who wants to get the most out of composting.

Equipment

Two square bins – each 1m by 1m (3ft by 3ft) at the bottom and 1.2–1.8m (4–6ft) high. You should be able to remove the front of the bin easily to enable turning over.

Fork

Thermometer – optional

Ingredients

Greens – vegetables, fruit, coffee grounds, tea leaves and bags (but not the don'ts – see pages 37–38 for a reminder), comfrey leaves, grass mowings, manure (without bedding), young weeds and plants, nettles, bracken, rhubarb leaves, strawy animal manures, cut flowers, soft hedge clippings, herbivore pet bedding, perennial weeds

Browns – old straw, tough vegetable stems, herbaceous stems, old bedding plants, autumn leaves (in small quantities), woody prunings, tough and evergreen hedge clippings, cardboard and paper, wood chip.

Guest List

Some like it hot and if you want to make sure these guys stick around for the whole course you're going to have to keep things steamy. No use cooling off on your guests halfway through. These composters are real swingers. They like nothing better than a spicy encounter in a sauna. These are the heat-loving, air-loving thermophilic micro-organisms.

Venue

For this you need to make the exactly proportioned compost bin described opposite.

Service

Medium Maintenance. To keep things going you'll have to turn the whole damn party over every three days. This seems to mix things up and fan the flames of revelry. Apart from that, you can leave them to it.

Preparation

If you're not already satiated from our main course, you've probably got a little bit of space for something from the dessert menu. We have a lovely pudding on offer – The Turnover. It's a real belt loosener, but not in the way you think.

In case you hadn't got it already, a Turnover is a compost heap that has to be turned over. By which I mean the contents moved from one bin to another and turned upside down; usually several times until the compost is ready. This obviously requires physical exertion on a scale not previously seen in *The Little Book of Compost*.

If composting were an Olympic sport, the Turnover would be the main event. This is competition compost, where speed, physical fitness and regular training make all the difference. Wonder what's the point of bothering if you've already got a perfectly good 'feed-and-forget' composting system?

Well, this is the pudding! And like all puddings, it's all a question of desire, belt capacity and the amount of ingredients you've got left in the cupboard. If you've got lots of energy for composting, a big garden filled with the kind of plants that require lots of compost (vegetables, fruit, demanding ornamentals) and lots of materials to compost then you're probably in need of a Turnover. If you've got a small garden with lots of decking, a few patio pot plants, a selection of undemanding plants and only a small amount of stuff to compost, then dessert might be off the menu.

The Turnover is completely different to all the other methods of composting described so far. For one thing, you have to start with a full bin. You don't add materials willy-nilly as they become available. You gather all the ingredients you need at the start and put them in the compost heap at the same time, not mixed up randomly, but carefully placed in alternating layers of browns and greens, one on top of the other. Whereas the others rise over time, this one shrinks.

A few days after you've constructed your wonderful compost heap, you destroy the construction by turning it over – usually into a second bin. This is because a Turnover has to be kept hot. And the only way to keep heat in a compost heap like this is to get air into every part of it. The only way to do that is to mix it up thoroughly by turning it over.

The hot compost heap is dominated by heat-loving, or thermophilic, micro-organisms. They are fast composters and decompose material quickly. Every time you turn a heap the air rushes in and metaphorically fans the flames inside. The composters get the air they need to carry on functioning and the pile stays hot.

As a general rule of thumb, the more you turn, the faster you compost. You are also far more likely to destroy all those weed seeds, roots and disease pathogens that linger in a cooler heap. For the dedicated gardener a hot compost heap provides certain guarantees of compost purity that don't really exist with cool composting. But, it does take more work, and this is the pay-off.

On the minus side, there is more work; on the plus side, more recycling, more compost and more guarantees. If, like most people, you want the plusses without the minuses there are a few ways to cheat – in other words to get lots of air into the heap without physically digging it all out. But none work quite as well as turning. One trick is to keep the compost raised above the ground and allow the air to rise into it. Another is to place lengths of perforated pipe through the heap so the air travels in and around. The last is probably the most convenient for the average household – to make or buy a bin with a turning handle. These are called tumbler bins and look a bit like an old-fashioned Tombola barrel. All the compost sits inside the tumbler and you just crank the handle round to turn the lot. *The Rodale Book of Compost* has DIY plans and full descriptions of all these short cuts.

The other disadvantage with the hot compost heap is that you need to more or less store ingredients up before you can start. Compost will not heat up without a prescribed critical mass of materials, so you need to accumulate the right proportions of green and brown material to start. This is fine when you have a regular supply of waste materials, although greens are almost always more available than browns, but not so good if it takes you weeks and weeks to get the requisite volumes of material to start a heap. I mean, what do you do with it while you're waiting to get enough? Compost it? Mmm.

One answer is to use household materials you might normally consider recycling. Cardboard and newspaper can be stored effectively in a garage or utility room and layered in a hot heap when you have enough greens to go with it. You could also chip prunings at the end of winter and store them in a pile for use as soon as spring throws up enough green materials to balance its brown-like qualities. On the green side of things, grass clippings are an obvious ready source of bulky nitrogenous materials.

In rural India, where the original Turnover recipe was cooked up by Englishman Sir Albert Howard, the hot compost heap combined endless amounts of vegetable wastes (a mixture of the greens and browns we talked about earlier, including straw, chaff, hay and clover, hedge and bank trimmings, weeds, prunings, bracken, leaves, sawdust, kitchen and other garden waste-nots) with animal dung (a nitrogen-rich green waste).

If you've gone self-sufficient-ish you could do the same with chicken, goat, pig and cow manure. You could even chuck in your rabbit poo. If it isn't enough, push back your garden gate and set out on to the open road. There's plenty of poo out there if you can be bothered to look for it. Some people get a bit obsessional about dung treasure hunts, cruising around their neighbourhood looking for the good stuff. They live in bungalows called Dung Roamin.

If you do get out and about, be eco, pick places that are close by, or combine your manure hunts with car journeys you already have to make. Otherwise you're just converting petrol into fertility, exactly what you're trying to avoid by not using chemical fertilisers. Better still, fix a trailer to your bike and peddle. Also, make sure you're getting the manure from animals that are treated to high welfare standards. Factory-farmed chicken manure is out. Personally, I wouldn't get manure from a non-organic farm either. Horse stables are a good place to look. They generally treat manure as a waste product so you might as well recycle it.

Of course, most of us, let's be realistic, aren't going to trail around the neighbourhood in a kind of Raiders of the Lost Fertility quest. We are either too lazy, too busy, too vegetarian or too Notting Hill. Personally, given the steepness and location of my garden the last thing I want to do is cart a load of dung there; especially as I'd have to hoik it through the house first. Whatever I compost has to come from within the garden or the house. If I want a little extra fertility, I head straight for the drinks menu before topping the whole meal off with a Wafer-thin Mint.

Method

Assemble critical mass of materials to fill a 1x1x1.2m (3x3x4ft) bin. You'll need two parts green to every one part brown. Put alternate layers of brown and green material in the bin – approximately 5cm (2in) of brown to every 10cm (4in) of green. It is good to mix up a variety of greens for each green layer and a variety of browns for each brown layer so the heap will get a balanced range of nutrients. If you've got big chunky bits of material to be composted cut them up so that they are no bigger than 15–20cm (6–8in) long. Stack the layers up so that the whole heap is between 1.2–1.8m (4–6ft) high. Leave the stack for two whole days. Over this time it will heat up considerably. On the third day turn the whole pile into the second bin so that the materials are all mixed. Make sure that the bits of compost on the outside of the bin are now right at the middle, where the micro-organisms are most active. Once you've turned the bin the layers you made will no longer be visible. After this first turn, turn the bin again on day six and day nine. On day 12 the compost should be ready for use, but if you're not sure it is, leave for a few days more and consider turning again.

Serving suggestions

Use in the same way as the recipe for Cold Turkey (see pages 23–32).

Cooking time

12 days, but allow more if the compost isn't ready.

Cook's Questions

I want to hot compost without turning, should I get a tumbler?

Tumblers are good for two basic scenarios:

- If you're short of space and you want all your composting to take place in a neat confined box you can keep in a yard or on a patio.

- If you don't want to fork over your compost heap.

Be warned, though: tumblers are not necessarily ultra easy on the muscles and bones. When they're full of compost, they're actually quite heavy and it takes some power to flip them over. If you can imagine turning over your entire hot compost heap in one go, you'll get an idea.

My advice is to see if you can try one out at a garden centre or garden visitor centre like the Garden Organic gardens or at CAT. Try to use a full one if you can.

They're also quite expensive. www.greengardener. co.uk sells the Tumbleweed Tumbler for about £100, but the most expensive tumbler I found was nearly £400.

You can make your own out of an old 55-gallon oil drum and a wooden turning platform. *The Rodale Book of Composting* contains full plans. You can buy this from www.cat.org.uk/shopping.

The Drinks Menu

May I interest you in a beverage? After all that Hot
Californian Turnover, you probably want a nice cup
of tea, or a cool refreshing cordial. Or at least
perhaps your plants do. Compost does a pretty good
job at getting the fertility your plants need back into
the soil, but sometimes it's useful to have an extra
source of nutrients that you can just pour on. This is
the theory behind most chemical fertilisers, which
come in a liquid feed and are simply applied to the
soil at certain times in the life cycle of a plant. But
chemical fertilisers take a lot of energy to produce
and are made using non-renewable resources. Why
buy in expensive fertilisers when we can make them
ourselves at home using plants grown in the garden?
This is where the Drinks Menu comes in.

Plants don't eat compost!

It used to be thought, a long time ago, that plants
ate compost, as if they had teeth on their roots.
Thanks to scientific enquiry, we now know that
plants absorb nutrients only when they are stored
in liquids. They cannot eat solid matter. In fact,

Golden Rule Alert
Sometimes compost isn't enough

At some point or other most gardeners metaphorically crash into the chemistry-inspired phrase NPK ratio. If, like me, you spent your chemistry lessons at school trying to work out how to send water up through the Bunsen burner this comes as quite a shock. What the deuce has chemistry got to do with gardening?

Well, actually quite a lot. Although most of this book has been about soil biology, there's also quite a lot of chemistry going on down there. All plant nutrients are chemicals and have their own chemical symbols. NPK stands for nitrogen (N), phosphorus (P) and potassium (K). Hang on a minute – K for potassium. You see, that's why I got so confused. Two p's and they call one of the p's K. Actually, it all makes sense when you know that the K is for Kalin, the Arabic word for potassium.

The NPK ratio represents the balance of key nutrients all plants need. Really it just means getting a balanced diet for plants. Just like the carbon–nitrogen ratio means getting a balanced diet for compost creatures. Worm casts have a good NPK ratio, as does most compost and comfrey liquid. Plants need a wide range of other nutrients apart from these three and can suffer deficiencies without them.

Apart from NPK there are four other major plant nutrients: calcium (Ca), magnesium (Mg), sulphur (S), Chlorine (Cl) and nine minor ones.

plants don't eat like we do at all. They create their own food by photosynthesising energy from the sun – the process converts sunlight into essential plant sugars (glucose). The nutrients they take from soil aid photosynthesis, and therefore the creation of energy and food. Without nutrients plants soon display signs of deficiency. In other words, they look ill.

To the naked eye, most soils and composts look like they're made up of pretty solid materials. When we pick up a handful of good soil we can feel that it is made up of crumbs – a bit like the mixture of flour and margarine in a crumble topping. What we can't see with the naked eye is the film of liquid that wraps itself around each crumb. This film of liquid is made up of water, micro-organisms and nutrients (see box opposite) – a small subterranean eco-system that supports everything else that goes on above.

The reason compost is so essential is that it keeps all this nutritious water locked in around the roots of the plant where it is needed most. It does this by helping tiny particles of soil that are too small to retain water to stick together to form larger crumbs.

As each crumb is capable of carrying its own sheath of water, the more crumbs there are in the soil, the more water there is. Soils full of compost will hold water longer in droughts and reduce the need for irrigation. Conventional gardens and farms using liquid feeds instead of compost will find that not only do they have to feed their plants more often, they also have to water them more often too. Plants in soils where there is no compost are more likely to wither and die unless they are continuously irrigated.

Conversely, compost also helps soils to drain more quickly in times of floods. Healthy soils full of compost have a good crumb structure with plenty of pockets and channels of air in between; many made by worms and other composter creatures when they move through the soil. These empty pockets and channels allow the water to flow easily.

So where does that leave us with our Drinks Menu? Well, let's take a swig and find out.

Compost Tea

Tetley for tomatoes. Poor Man's Brew.

This one's for:

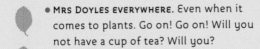

- **MRS DOYLES EVERYWHERE.** Even when it comes to plants. Go on! Go on! Will you not have a cup of tea? Will you?

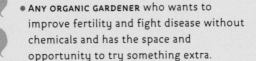

- **ANY ORGANIC GARDENER** who wants to improve fertility and fight disease without chemicals and has the space and opportunity to try something extra.

Budget
You can pay over £100 for a pumped compost tea maker or use an old bucket you have lying around.

Equipment
One bucket

Ingredients
Good home-made compost you're confident
contains lots of micro-organisms. You won't be
able to see them unless you've got an electron-
microscope kicking around so you're just going
to have to have faith on this one. Don't use bought
bagged compost. These are usually sterilised and
free of micro-organisms.

Cool water (preferably of the rain variety). This is
a cold tea.

Guest List
By this point in the meal most of the composters
have faded away, moved on to something more
happening, but right here at the end there are
still a few contenders. The air-loving, cool-loving
micro-organisms are there. They love a nice cup
of tea. But what's this? Just waiting in the wings
hoping to make another appearance, looking
enviously at the drinks list are our rummy friends
the anaerobic digesters. Never ones to droop,
they'll do anything to turn an innocent little brew
into something stronger. Mash it up, they say,
but this time you have to stir things up yourself

to keep them away. They're no good for making compost tea and you need to keep mixing the brew to get plenty of air in there.

Venue
This is perhaps one of the least glamorous party venues – a five-gallon bucket will do, or a neglected water butt. You don't have to slum it though. If you start taking the science of tea making seriously you might want to splash out on something more sumptuous.

Service
Medium Maintenance. So long as they've got enough air they'll be happy.

Preparation
The theory is simple enough. Plants only take nutrients in liquid form. Why not let the nutrients in compost steep in a tea and feed the tea direct to the soil? The practice is slightly more complicated.

When you make compost tea you're actually trying to rinse the micro-organisms out of the compost and into the tea, so the starting point is always good compost full of all the good aerobic micro-organisms we've been talking about (bacteria, fungi, protozoa, nematodes). If you start out with good compost you have a good chance of making good compost tea.

Like all tea making the secret to a good brew is matching the volume of water to the volume of tea (the compost) and knowing when to whip the bag out. There's only so much oxygen in water and micro-organisms soaked in water quickly use up what's available. If you start making compost tea with too little water and too much compost the tea goes anaerobic. The air-loving organisms loved so much by plants die and are replaced by anaerobic organisms that may be harmful to both our plants and us. Conversely, there is no point dipping the bag in gingerly for a weak tea. It takes between 12 and 24 hours to get a good brew going. A day is a long time in the life of a micro metropolis and the number of micro-organisms can quadruple in compost tea.

When you've made your brew you can spray it on the leaves of your plants as well as pouring it into the soil. Because the micro-organisms in compost tea are very effective at dealing with other micro-organisms that are harmful to plants – as well as providing fertility – they help to inoculate plants against attack from pests and diseases.

Despite its rather homely name making compost tea is cutting-edge science and it pays to get it right. When you apply a really good compost tea to the leaves of your plants or to the soil you're adding an entire food web of micro-organisms that will do battle on your behalf with all the soil nasties. If part of the food web is missing because the process hasn't worked as well as it might, you're not getting the full benefit. On the other hand you get what you pay for, and in this case you pay quite a lot. If you're a really keen organic gardener growing a lot of fruit and veg in a large garden, it's probably worth making the investment. Before you do anything, read about compost tea on www.soilfoodweb.com. They provide full instructions on how compost tea works and a list of authorised US-based compost tea makers.

Method

Fill one quarter of the bucket with compost. Fill the rest with water. Stir several times during the next 24–48 hours. Make and use compost tea at intervals of between 10 and 14 days.

Serving suggestions

Dilute the resultant liquid to a light amber colour and pour 600ml (1 pint) around each plant when you're planting out.

Cooking time

24–48 hours plus the time it takes to make the compost.

Cook's Questions

Where can I buy a compost tea maker?

Most bought compost tea makers keep air moving through the tea by using an electric pump. It's quite difficult to buy a pumped compost tea maker in Britain. I couldn't find one. In the States www.soilfoodweb.com have set standards for compost tea makers and have a wide range to choose from. Some of these are big-scale agricultural tea makers but some are more suitable for gardeners. If you can't find a pumped compost tea maker you can make your own using a bucket, tubes, valves, air stones and a small aquarium air pump – see www.mdvaden.com/compost_tea.shtml for details. These obviously use fuel, so make sure you're buying your electricity from a green supplier. www.soilfoodweb.com suggest that compost tea makers without pumps do not produce teas with the same range of bacterial activity. In the UK, you can buy a non-pumped compost tea maker made by Envirocomp UK (www.envirocompuk.net) from CAT (www.cat.org.uk/shopping).

Comfrey Cordial

This one's for:

- **ANYONE WHO LIKES THE IDEA OF GROWING PLANTS** to improve fertility rather than using chemicals and who needs to give pot-bound, greenhouse and plants in poor soil a boost of instant nitrogen.

There are lots of ways to make comfrey cordial. Alan Titchmarsh shows you one at www.crocus.co.uk; search under 'make your own plant food'. Garden Organic another at www.organicgarden.org.uk/growing/grow/comfpress.htm. Here's a third.

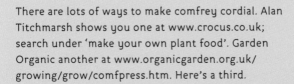

Budget
You'll need about £10 to get your comfrey roots and growing instructions.

Equipment

There's two ways to go with this simple comfrey cordial recipe. One is to buy a Bokashi bin or something else with a tap, forget about Bokashi composting and just fill it with comfrey leaves. The other is to get a bucket, put a hole in the bottom and raise it above the ground so the liquid can drip into a second smaller bucket or container underneath. Either way you need to weigh down your comfrey leaves with something brick like to squeeze the liquid out. It helps to cut a piece of wood the size of the base of the bucket to stand the brick on inside the bucket. That way you can put your hand round the brick and press down on all the comfrey in the bucket.

If you're going for the 'there's a hole in my bucket' approach, you'll need to make a stand on which to place your bucket. A couple of old breeze blocks will do it, or recycled bricks or other solid material you might have lying around. So long as you leave enough room underneath the bucket for the smaller bucket, it doesn't really matter how it stays up. Having said that, make sure it doesn't fall over when you try to retrieve your liquid. No comfrey-pressed fingers please!

Ingredients
Mature comfrey leaves cut at six-week intervals complete with stems and flowers. Chuck the lot in.

Guest List
Now the anaerobics get their chance. The last hurrah!

Venue
A selection of choice buckets. See below.

Service
Low maintenance. In fact, no maintenance.

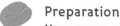

Preparation

Mmmmmmm comfrey. If you're a fan of *The Simpsons* picture me at my desk with a glazed look in my eye and a cascade of dribble sliding over my chin towards QWERTY. Comfrey to Allan the composter is donut with double caramel topping to Homer the fridge raider. This is a mouth-watering treat of a plant. It's easy to grow, perfect to compost and great to turn into a liquid feed.

It is what you might call big-boned. A big-leaved big green plant that doesn't particularly sit well in the average flower border. If you were being unkind, you could call it ugly; slightly Shrek like. It's tough and prickly, and as it can irritate skin, not that kid-friendly.

On the other hand, those big ugly leaves are packed full of nutrients, sucked up by enormous brutish roots from deep soils. Cut them down, compost them or turn them into a liquid feed and you're redistributing soil wealth to those plants that need it most. Gordon Brown would probably like the term given to this process – dynamic accumulation. Comfrey is one of the best dynamic accumulators in the business, bringing up from deep soils silica, nitrogen, magnesium, calcium, potassium and iron and making them available to other less fortunately rooted but tastier plants.

Comfrey has a good carbon-nitrogen ratio – about ten to one – and an excellent NPK ratio; it is, all in all, a great plant to turn into a liquid fertiliser.

Growing comfrey is easy. You should buy the variety Bocking 14 from The Organic Gardening Catalogue (www.organiccatalog.com) and follow the instructions provided by Garden Organic's step-by-step guide to growing comfrey. The catalogue will send you both for less than £7.50 plus postage.

Method

Whether you go for bucket or Bouquet, the theory is the same. Chuck the comfrey in. Put the piece of wood on top of the comfrey. Put the brick on top of that. Press down. Add another brick if you need to stop the comfrey bouncing back up. Shut the lid. Leave. Wait. Within a few weeks the comfrey should turn from leaf to liquid. If you want to, you can give it a squeeze with the brick now and then to encourage it along. If you're using a Bokashi bucket, the liquid will fall into the sump, from which it can be extracted via the tap. If you're using the holed bucket, you'll see when it's ready. It will start dripping into the drip bucket.

Serving suggestions

Like any other cordial, this one needs watering down. Garden Organic recommend one part comfrey concentrate to every fifteen parts of water. Comfrey cordial has the right balance of plant food for tomatoes, peppers and French beans and can be used more generally for other greenhouse crops, pot plants and outdoor crops where access to good deep compost-filled soils is limited. It is possible to over-feed crops using liquid fertilisers so a little research is needed before you start using it. Plants have different needs throughout their lives and it may be appropriate to only use the feed at a particular time in the life cycle. Tomatoes for example do not need feeding when they are very young but by the time they're covered in fruit require a thrice-weekly dose. Go to the Garden Organic website (www.gardenorganic.org.uk) and type 'comfrey liquid feed' in the search engine for some great tips about how much to feed plants, where and when.

Cooking Time
About one month.

Cook's Questions
Can I buy liquid feeds?
Many gardeners buy liquid feeds when it becomes clear their plants are lacking certain nutrients and perhaps suffering illness or slow growth as a result, either because they are grown in containers without access to a reliable variety of nutrients or on poor soils. Various organic fertilisers are available – made from liquid manures, fish emulsion, rock phosphate and a variety of other plant extracts, including vinasse, sugar beet and seaweed. Most are especially formulated to remedy specific deficiencies, so check your growing instructions first and follow the instructions on the label. Whilst you're staring at the label, check for the Soil Association symbol; this ensures you're buying a product that is made using the highest organic standards. Make sure you don't buy a chemical fertiliser by mistake! Check out www.organiccatalog.com, go to the Soil and Plant Care section, then the Feeding page.

Are there other liquid feeds I can make at home?
Yes. You can make a very good liquid feed out of
nettles using the same method as for comfrey. And
then there is, of course, that most home-made of all
nitrogen fertilizers – urine. A cheeky little sherry
we produce every day, which generally gets sent
down the toilet but could be used to feed our plants.
You have to dilute urine before you water it on your
garden – ten parts of water to one part urine is a
sensible mix. It doesn't add anything to the structure
of the soil, but it does boost plant growth. Before
trying it read up on the subject (try *Liquid Gold*
by Carol Steinfeld) and have a listen to my podcast
interview with self-confessed urine nerd Peter
Harper of CAT. You can download it from my blog
www.compostlover.com or from iTunes.

The Wafer-thin Mint

This one is for

 ● ALL GOOD GARDENERS EVERYWHERE

This is not composting as we know it, which is why it's represented in *The Little Book of Compost* as the wafer-thin mint at the end of the meal, but it is composting. There are no buckets and bins. No turning or stirring. No mixing browns and greens. Just a handful of carefully selected green manure plants grown for their ability to make, or fix, nitrogen out of thin air and then cut to improve the fertility and the structure of the soil.

Although it comes at the end of the book disguised as a wafer-thin mint, this method of composting is just as important as all the other recipes. This is because it marks the point when you move beyond being a great compost chef and start becoming a master of the soil.

Equipment

As this is a recipe for growing crops, you'll need at least a **rake** and probably a **fork** to prepare the bed in which you will be planting your green manures. There are several nitrogen-generating, or to use the horticultural term, nitrogen-fixing green manures and each requires a slightly different method of cultivation and cropping. Some are left to grow tall. For these you'll need a **cutting device** like a pair of secateurs, a scythe or a sickle. Others can be hoed back into the soil or dug in and chopped up with a spade.

Ingredients

Green manure seeds: alfalfa, field beans, crimson clover, other clovers, lupins, tares, trefoil. Order from any of the following:

- www.organiccatalog.com, look under Seeds then Green Manures (0845 1301304)
- www.suffolkherbs.com (01376 572456)

- www.edwintucker.com (01364 652233)
- www.tamarorganics.co.uk (01579 371087),
- www.beansandherbs.co.uk/greenmanures

Guest list

Bacteria from the Rhizobia clan are the only ones who can fix nitrogen from the air and they can only do it when they enter the roots of a legume: beans, peas, pulses, peanuts, vetches, lupins, Lucerne and clover. They actually go through a metamorphosis inside the root, creating a nodule in which they morph into a shape we call a bacteroid. Only when they become a bacteroid can they start to take nitrogen from the air and make it available to the plant. What it gets back from the plant is a share of the sugars created by photosynthesis. It uses them to grow and multiply. It is one of those magical symbiotic moments where plant and bacteria come together to do something wonderful – create fertility that wouldn't otherwise exist, both for them and the plants and other organisms around them.

Venue

The vegetable plot: in real soil; no buckets or bin; straight in the ground.

Service

Low maintenance. After the seeds are sown there's not much more to do. Let the crop grow to the required height, cut down and dig back into the soil.

Preparation, Method and Serving Suggestion

Green manures are primarily used in the vegetable garden as part of a four-course rotation (see Cook's Questions below). They are planted between rows or when ground is left empty over winter or after a crop is lifted. They can also be left in the soil over several years when the area needs to recover from overuse. They provide a ground cover to suppress weeds, increase nitrogen levels in the soil and provide food for our cool-loving, air-loving micro-organisms. This keeps worms and the like happy and they, in turn, maintain good soil structure.

They're easy to grow but you'll need a guide to using them properly. Try one of the following:

- Garden Organic's leaflet *Green Manures: step-by-step guide* (£1.35 from www.organiccatalog.com)
- The quick guide at www.gardenorganic. org.uk/factsheets/gs3.php.

- or the more in-depth one at www.veganorganic.net/images/greenmanur es.pdf (0845 223 5232).

Once you've read up, order your seeds and start planting.

Cooking Time
From three months to several years, depending on which crop and why you are growing them.

Cook's questions
Are green manures pretty and do they have any wildlife value?
Some green manures are prettier than others and will look good in a non-formal or semi-naturalistic border. Their flowers are also attractive to bees and other pollinating insects – although green manures are often cut before they flower.

What is a four-course rotation and why is it important?
Vegetables are demanding plants. If you grow them in the same space year after year, the soil around them tends to suffer from a build-up of pests and diseases. Rotating crops so that they only occupy the same patch of soil once every four years reduces

this risk and allows you to treat the soil in different ways to meet the specific needs of the vegetables you are growing.

Vegetables are divided into tribes of species that need similar conditions to grow. The big four tribes are Solanaceae and Cucurbitaceae (potatoes, courgettes, pumpkins and tomatoes); legumes (peas and beans); brassicas (cabbages, Brussels sprouts, broccoli); and root crops (carrots, beetroot, parsnips). The legume crop gives the soil a much needed additional nitrogen boost once every four years.

Conclusion

So there we have it, a seven-course meal with a little something extra at the end to keep your guests happy as they leave. There's lots more to composting and soil fertility than I could hope to cram into this little book but I hope its provided you with the best starting point you could want. Use the Ideas Larder to carry on learning and most important of all: Bon Appetite!

The Ideas Larder

Now that you're going to become a regular compost chef, you'll need a little larder full of useful resources. Here it is!

Key Contacts

YOUTUBE – INTERNET VIDEO SITE WWW.YOUTUBE.COM is full of home-made videos of people composting – some of them slightly bizarre but many of them useful. Type in a key word like Bokashi, or wormery or composting, and see what comes up. The videos are always changing, but if they're still there when you're looking, I'd recommend the following

- Kindergarten Composting
- Worm Composting
- Coffee to Compost
- How to Make a Compost Bin in Under Two Minutes

ALLAN SHEPHERD: WWW.COMPOSTLOVER.COM
This is my blog. You'll find useful information and news about what I'm doing, including details of my podcast and lots of good stuff about organic gardening.

Centre for Alternative Technology: www.cat.org.uk; 01654 705950

An amazing place to find out how to live a green life. Their mission is to inspire, inform and enable. You can visit CAT for a day, take a course, volunteer, come with your school for a week, join the membership group or just browse the website. Here you'll find loads of free information and tonnes of really good eco books and products available through mail order. They're also the publisher of a wide range of books, including several of mine (see below).

Garden Organic: www.gardenorganic.org.uk; 024 7630 3517

Gardening resource for organic gardeners with three visitor centres, educational facilities, information service and membership and research programmes.

Gardening Which? magazine; www.which.co.uk/gardeningwhich; 0800 252100

Great resource for gardeners. Have occasional special issues on composting in which composting methods and bins are tested. Recently came out in favour of the 'feed and forget' composting method as the best for most gardeners – although they did turn their heap once every two months for good measure.

GREEN GARDENER: WWW.GREENGARDENER.CO.UK;
01603 715096
Supplies a wide range of compost goodies.

Organic Gardening MAGAZINE:
WWW.ORGANICGARDENINGMAGAZINE.CO.UK; 01507 529529
Best UK gardening magazine for organic methods.
Includes in-depth features on techniques, news
round-ups and book reviews.

ORGANIC GARDENING CATALOGUE:
WWW.ORGANICCATALOG.COM; 0845 1301304
Supplier of a wide range of composting equipment,
liquid feeds and fertilisers, ready-made compost and
lots of other gardening books and products.

RECYCLE NOW:
WWW.RECYCLENOW.COM/HOME__COMPOSTING;
0845 077 0757
Government-backed website for recycling and
composting. Highly recommended as an excellent
source of information for all composters.

RECYCLE WORKS: WWW.RECYCLEWORKS.CO.UK;
01254 820088
Specialist mail order service supplying a wide range
of compost goodies.

WIGGLY WIGGLERS: WWW.WIGGLYWIGGLERS.CO.UK
0800 216990
Specializes in worms and wormeries but also supplies a wide range of composting and wildlife gardening goodies.

Further reading

IN PRINT

An Ear to the Ground: Garden Science for Ordinary Mortals, Ken Thompson, Eden Books

Cool Composting, Peter Harper, Centre for Alternative Technology Publications

Growing Green: Organic Techniques for a Sustainable Future, Jenny Hall and Iain Tolhurst, The Vegan Organic Network

HDRA Encyclopedia of Organic Gardening, Editor-in-Chief Pauline Pears, Dorling Kindersley

Liquid Gold, Carol Steinfeld, Green Books

Organic Gardening: The Natural No-Dig Way, Charles Dowding, Green Books

Start with the Soil, Grace Gershuny, Rodale Press

Soil Food: 1372 Ways to add fertility to your soil, Jackie French, Aird Books

Teaming with Microbes: A Gardeners' Guide to the Soil Food Web, Jeff Lowenfels and Wayne Lewis

Wild Solutions: How diversity is money in the bank, Andrew Beattie and Paul R. Ehrlich, Yale University Press

The Organic Garden, Allan Shepherd, Collins

The Little Book of Garden Heroes, Allan Shepherd, Centre for Alternative Technology Publications

The Little Book of Garden Villains, Allan Shepherd, Centre for Alternative Technology Publications

The Rodale Book of Composting, Edited by Deborah Martin and Grace Gershuny, Rodale

The Worm Book, Loren Nancarrow and Janet Hogan Taylor, Ten Speed Press

Weeds: An Earth-friendly Guide to their Identification, Use and Control, John Walker, Daily Telegraph and Cassell illustrated

OUT OF PRINT BUT AVAILABLE SECOND HAND – TRY THE MARKET PLACE ON WWW.AMAZON.CO.UK

An Agricultural Testament, Sir Albert Howard, Other India Press

Fertility without Fertilisers, Lawrence D. Hills (HDRA)

Comfrey: Past, Present and Future, Lawrence D.Hills, Faber

The Gardener's Practical Botany, John Tampion, David and Charles

The World of the Soil, Sir E. John Russell, Collins

Index

Acknowledgements

I'd like to thank Chloe Ward for continuing to fill my own gardening ideas larder; my editors at Collins, Jenny Heller and Lizzy Gray; my designers Emma Ewbank and Bob Vickers; and my colleagues at the Centre for Alternative Technology, in particular Caroline Oakley, Graham Preston, Christian Hunt and Marcus Zipperlen. I'd also like to thank Sian Jones at Waterstones for starting the whole thing off and Jamie Blanchfield at Garden Organic.